THE FIRE

The Fire by Lorenzo Lago

Copyright 2015, 2026

Correspondence: www.lorenzolago.com

Cover Art: *The Fisherman and the Syren: From a Ballad by Goethe,*

1857 (oil on canvas), Leighton, Frederic (1830-96) / © Bristol Museum and Art Gallery, UK / Bridgeman Images

ISBN# 9780692428672

THE FIRE

Dedicated to all who cherish jumping into The FIRE.

Lorenzo Lago

TABLE OF CONTENTS

AUTHOR'S NOTE

Water, salted and fresh…

Spending my life around the ocean has influenced what I've written about for decades. Surfing and the saltwater baptism is forever being revitalized in my life. I love that I get to go surfing.

Along with this ocean energy, I honor my place among all nature's elements, those of fire, earth, air and water. It's amazing how special these aspects are in my life, as of most lives.

In addition to prose about the ocean's heavy vitality, I've included poetic narratives in this manuscript about a treasured lake, high in the mountains of Northern California, that I have frequented the last few summers. I love paddling my Stand-Up-Paddleboard across the glassy liquid, and also being able to swim in the lake's warm water. I am so grateful for this experience. The lake, and the time spent in and around it, has been a life-enhancing encounter.

I have to thank my good friend, Steve Quirt, for advising me to go with the first version of the poem, 'Wild Mountain Honey!'and omit the second, more subdued copy. After I digested the original poem, I assessed the piece to be too lush, just too seductively powerful for my reading audience. So I created a second, mellower version of the poem. I eased the savage tone the poem evokes. This, of course, could never work, as I can only write from my heart. Wild Mountain Honey! does flaunt the reader with the sensual! So the hell with the second version! I feel that the sexiness and bravado of the poem's words bestow a beautiful image. So, thanks amigo for reminding me to be true to myself.

Romance is so beautiful an expression of love that we might as well release the wild, and let that untamed thrill become a dazzling explosion! Make it poetic, enhance, and savor the emotion. Illuminate the senses, ignite the fire, and let it burn!

YOUNG AT HEART

A STRONG CURRENT

I believe the season of spring is upon my life
For here, the current flows as a kiss
Its caress teases, I am flattered

To have travelled the world, chasing the sun
And to at last, find an impassioned shore
One, whose melody springs forth from a dark sea lament,
or that evening trail, where I had no choice, but to lose my way
Oh, how I have tired of the search

This new shore, it is one of illumination
This sparkling current,
as if suspended from the stars, feeds my soul

This reflection, has now become my chant
Sung like the celebrated emergence of dawn,
or a night of a seasoned moon, full and timeless

Yes, this new dawning has opened my heart

I believe the season of spring is upon my life

POETRY APPEARS

Unwrap the thoughts that become words,
unfold the images
Move from an obscure reflection, to a distinct package

Satiate verses
Let them surge out from that hidden space
That sacred zone, that lies deep inside

Allow those words to slowly ooze back into your heart…
And, after hours, no much more…
months of editing,
ultimately,
stanzas, unquenched, and correct, fill the pages

This is how it begins, and closes

ANCHORED

I drift with the wind, but this pulling at my heart lingers
My soul aches to rest in my home
To be safe from any, and all intrusion

This constant yearning to be back in port
The vessel shut down tight, resting dockside
Far from the wind, the inclement weather, the wild sea
No dragons of the deep searching for me

+++

Only to drive toward home…
To pilot that last street, turn the car engine off, and to heed the quiet
I long to step into the night air, calm in breath, and whisper, "Home at last"

I yearn to rest by the hearth, and to savor its comforting warmth
To grasp this reassurance, and to be so thankful

I crave to be near my lover
Her head, resting upon my chest
Her body, to cover my eternity

+++

Wandering no more… it's good to be home

BACK IN THE OCEAN

I surf as much as possible.

If conditions are right, there is no other place I'd rather be, than in the ocean and riding waves. It's engrained in my spirit. So why not let my spirit expand?

Most everyday, the same usual faces are in the water. Each of us, in our own style, gracefully float with waves, actually dance on moving salt water. And what a dance floor! I get to share this surfing experience with diverse acquaintances, and with different generations, young and old. We are having fun, and staying fit. Just riding waves. There is really no other place I'd rather be.

I surf as much as possible.

BACK TO THE POOL

I swim daily.

At the university pool, I see acquaintances of our swim tribe. There is a different vibe here than those I surf alongside. It's not at all an unhappy setting, we just don't know each other very well. We just happen to meet at our place of refuge on a regular basis. There's usually an acknowledgement, a small hello, but no real socializing. This is fine, as we all share a common goal and understanding. Yes, we are all here getting our fix. Just taking care of our 'submerging in liquid' habit. Each one of us, in our own way, is sending our spirit into a *zone* that is free. It's a simple way to release everything, and surge ahead in life. Swimming is our tangible, and rewarding way of blasting off!

I swim daily.

SPIRIT SURF

Spirit Surf, how you encompass my soul!
Gliding free across waves
Soaring for decades of thrilling rides

+++

We drop anchor, and stow what's necessary
Born in some forgotten dream, robust waves break across the tropic reef
Each wave is magnificent, and so ready to be ridden!

My surfboard is the perfect brush for this expression of riding art
Liquid moving art…

+++

Here I go…paddling into the line-up…direct into this deep profound energy!

Driving down the face, and I accelerate into my turn, and fly across the
canvas!
Full speed, I glide the length of the blue…

THE TRADE WINDS ARE HOWLING TONIGHT!

I know that this swell will not to back off
Sets of waves will march through
It will be a day filled with memorable turns, and stylish trimming

Each ride will be exaggerated
Filled with exuberance!

Time for laughs, laybacks, and being launched!

So inspiring! So, sacred!

THE INVITATION

Sunbeams of strength filter through the forest

Light lingers, swallows and cradles the harmony

This land of trees
Transecting a clever fabric of age
Patterns with taste and perfect fashion

It's art, it's an oath, the rite of passage

CHILD

grand sacrament of birth
a new face to look upon the world
a new soul to quench its thirst

mother and father will do their best
love will rest upon their chest

little one, you make sense
such clear innocence

you will find your way into all hearts

EARLY RAIN

Last night, a soft rain whispered lightly
Awakening the hour before the dawn, my half-opened window summoned
A gently calm descended from heaven, and floated down from the sky

I lay in bed listening to the raindrops tap against the soil
The sprinkling of moisture declared to sustain the earth, and myself
At this early hour, a nourishing morning aura is present

Life's going well, things are aligning, and life's thriving
There's a sense of elation within my world

Maybe, it's just some days, things align better then we expect
I am thankful the Universe does that at times…

The world out there, the one that can be difficult
I figure, you just have to settle into your own bliss
All the other stuff, is just stuff, and you just have to deal with it

My cheerful spirit, must be because of how much I relish my home, here on
the coast
This abode, what a treasure
It's grand when these special gifts appear when we need them most
I'm thankful the Universe does that at times…

I feel settled here, ready to remain for an extended phase
Yes, this is an agreeable place to breathe with ease

The last few years were filled with travels, surfing and composing verse
Catching my breath for some months, and more surfing and writing
transpiring

Those in-between houses, were all snug and secure,
but now, I dwell in Lorenzo's Villa
Not really a villa, more a small cottage, but ideal for me

I mentioned to a friend, that all I need is to have a woman in the house
Attractive, and running around half-naked, spreading her feminine qualities a
muck. That would indeed make this home complete. The addition of a Venus
femme would indeed enhance and illuminate the household

Perhaps one day, she will appear…
Believe me, her presence will be exquisite, celestial and honored

I better stoke up the fireplace with some oak, seasoned true
I have to make sure my home is inviting for her anticipated arrival

RED LEAVES

Drunk with Autumn wisdom

the maple tree turns its face to the season

all influence flushed ruby red

FATHER TREES

The river gentle turns and winds its way toward the lake's full body
Its design, blushed with exploration for all who are here this morning

+++

Poetic strokes, and a flat-water glide
I float the surface, and move with the even flow
Liquid space of bliss

I love the long expanse to the other side of the lake
So many dreamy coves to explore

Easy of breath, stretch on spirit
My glide takes me into heaven

Alive, the lake resonates
How clear, and how precise, nature displays itself

+++

The Father Trees, they tower above families of flora
Each tree appears so graceful
Harmonic resonance within the forest colors
It's trance like, mesmerizing

+++

My return toward home

Absolute, unlimited and complete

BODY OF WATER

Poetic strokes, I transverse the water's expanse to the far shore
So many coves to Huck Finn

Sacred water, rich in creation, you echo the valley
Your heart swirls the shallows, and the deep

Ushered upon the blue,
I glide the water's surface and seize the harmony within

I hear you, I know you

GRAVITY AND MAGNETISM

It's all about gravity and magnetism
Lacking it, we would have nothing

Without the Law of Gravity, we would just float away
   just drift off…
there'd be nothing but space, only space!

And, it's Magnetism that keeps us settled here on the ground
   Among the family, among the tribes
Without it, we would have nothing

It is flawless science, flawless faith, fascinating and absolute

NOCTURNAL GUEST

Lustrous gem of the night, hushed glimpse in soft white
My lustrous friend, you help a heart to mend

Floating through scattered cloud, you emerge big and proud
Digesting the sky, so onward you fly

+++

Goodbye moon, you've grown tired
So, cover your face, and disappear from the race

Such is the magical lore,
I believe you'll arrive once more

+++

Oh, how the fabled moon can rouse the dreamy poet's verse

HALF-WAY

"Hey, how you doing? Is that some kind of kayak?"

I observed the fellow who asked. I couldn't tell how old he was, but he seemed to be of high school age. It was the braces on his teeth that had me thinking he was a teenager.

"Half-way there," he declared, smiling through the silvery covering.

It felt good to see another soul this warm, August morning.

"No, this is a Stand-Up-Paddleboard," I answered.

He observed my craft, checking the lines of its design.

"Looks like a good way to explore the lake," he remarked.

"Yeah, I love it!" was all I could declare. Followed by, "Half-way?"

"Yes," he smiled through his silver. "I'm walking around the lake, should take a while, but loving the trek! I'm seeing all kinds of neat things!"

"Have a great one!" I remarked, and recognized that I had just met another colleague of the 'tribe'.

I guess we're all half-way there…
From our birth…through our end. Or from a beginning…to another beginning. Perhaps, half-way in the middle of a friendship, an awareness, a romance, or a lifetime.

I like the half-way point. I feel I have an appropriate perspective on what this Universe is all about. Life that is.

Who knows, am I only half-way there, or just beginning, or near some kind of ending?

I imagine, that I am just half way there.

MORNING HIKE

The forest alive with a golden morning sun
  its earthen soil covered with the wet glow of pine needles
    grey streaks of disappearing clouds float up mountain valleys
      alas, a grand solar ashram floods the canyon walls like a symphony

I travel light
  agile and quiet
    no marching legion to disrupt the pristine
      deep within the earth's presence, there is a song for this day
        whispering a melody,
          for those that revel in this impressive display of nature

I trek the high ridge
  down through the mountain pass
    beside hilly expanse
      among spring meadows
        between brush, thick with sticky vines and sculptured branches
          each with its own integrity

Fertile fields fill with imagination
Each flushed flower gives way to the seasons

And now, resting along the river's edge,
  I bathe in its sweet water

MOONLIT MOUNTAIN

Out, beyond the open door
  an evening of April
    its hallowed warm air spreads across my life

Puddles of water fill steps of spring,
  for a light tender rain lingers
An eternal mountain sky,
    washed clean

There,
  proud tree of Pine
  lyrical Manzanita
      both, soothe this night
Their branches gently sway to the breeze
      between an honored new moon
Ah, look, Venus, the shy planet

Adrift in these hours
loyal expert, mentor
breath of my soul, charmed trance of this life

I so honor this sacred ceremony

HAPPY PROSE

mouth
    stuffed
        happy

bits
    of
        chocolate chip cookie

crumble
    to
        the
            floor

OH, THE DAY

I surge
    past the cosmos
        this is the life to live!

STAY OPTIMISTIC, SURF ON

what, no way!
    screw that!
        I'm going surfing!

ASCENDING

Like the hawk…
    I soar
        above
            and beyond

SURFINGGYPSY.COM

It's been so calm on the ocean's surface
    Hardly a speck of wind
    If any breeze, just a wisp of offshores
The sea is smiling

The waves have been playful, and I've been playing
    Two or three go-outs each day
Almost surfed out, but not quite

Some food, rest, and on it again!
    This is the life I've succumbed too…the vagabond's lifestyle, the beach life

The muse, and its seductive song within the waves

HUSH-HUSH

Small secrets are sacred
   Those hidden shores of radiance
The places and people, the romances, the secret surf sites

The circumstance, so exceptional, so holy,
   that it should never be uttered, and to anyone
Revealing such secrets, it's like letting go of a sacred breath

You know in your heart you should have never uttered a word,
   but then it's too late, and the story is now revealed
The lost art of keeping a secret is so significant!

Perhaps someday, the secret is to be shared to someone special
   Yes, what of those people, the extra special friends
   The tribe that is from the same spiritual space we live
They'll honor the secret

Those open windows with value,
   serenades of vistas,
   private earth meadows
That secluded beach, hidden from most,
   so pure and fine with its grains of bleached sand, white with antiquity

Yes, this corner of the lake, and the bay that lies so tranquil at sunset…
Oh, you really want to share this, offer this gift to one who appreciates this
absolute

Maybe you are revealing these secrets?
  Exposing fields and flower rainbows
  Illuminating essential places that your heart holds so dear,
    for this is the moment to impart the awe to that treasured friend

This is quite a gift to share
  These places that deserve a standing ovation
    That embody truth and friendship, and carry blessed embers

Some mysteries should never be divulged
  Yet some surprises, those of distinction, I think they're meant to be disclosed

Either way, small secrets are sacred

PERU

My host and daughter,

  and my great love for you

We are family,

  we are of one tribe

Your mystic connection to these mountains,

  this sacred valley of magic,

    is so full with understanding

I wouldn't want to feel these mountains,

  this valley, in any other way,

    but to have you near, showing me all you have to share

RAIN

Throughout the day

    puddles of rainwater

        launch paths of fraternal mazes

Farmers laugh through porcelain mugs of dark coffee

Water

    falls

        like tears

            across old dry newspapers

I sit

    stargazing

        through a window wet with words

FEAR

This forest is filled with darkness
It's so damn deep in darkness!
I'm unfamiliar with this space
This forest dwells in a sky that my true nature won't accept

+++

Although you knew it was inevitable,
   your lover declares that she wants out of the bond
Or perhaps, you confess, it's you that needs change,
   and you're first to break a heart
+
The business investment. The one that didn't flourish
Thousands of dollars vanishing in a day
   And only, to return in the form of debt
+
The phone call, that you never expect
A nurse from the doctor's office, informing you that ya now have cancer
   I have what?

+++

This is the time to punch the energy reload button!
This is when you dive deep into your mind and your spirit…
You tell yourself, and everyone else…
   "I'll ride this wave, however unfortunate it is, with style and grace"
         (I love those surfing metaphors)

The reality of 'fear' does catch us off guard
The Universe decides to mess with our peace of mind
    Health, love, money…time to unravel!

+++

Luckily our true spirit, my true spirit, rises in earnest
    Time to defend the galaxy (nerves and neurons)!

Yeah, the light of awareness, tells fear to go fuck itself!

My Friend, my advice…
    Become a warrior, and overcome the foe
Live for as long as you can, and with gusto!

Grab your board, and go for a surf! And, ride it with style and grace!

TRUTH WARRIOR

Within this immortal display of nature
I glide
   fearless, across valleys of moon sand
   carried onward, floating on celestial footsteps
   inside a vortex of integrity

It's brilliance, so shining
   so sincere
    it points in my direction

I shed a skin of indifference
   and flee a world where sanity and sainthood scratch my eyes like a virus
I will build a fire where the hearth glows infallible
   its embers, shall be shells of emotional ammunition

My star of truth, rectified with a compass of faith
   It is time to care for my heart, as all hearts

It's my voyage on this forever road, and there will be no stormy sky at my
doorstep

BLEACH WHITE, SAPPHIRE BLUE

Machete in hand, and two hours of marching this jungle,
I'm wondering if this trek is worth the effort
I didn't feel this way an hour ago, but that was an hour ago!
This relentless heat has seized my easy-going attitude, and thrown it over a
cliff!

All this, and for a wave!

You do this kind of trekking when 'surf' is in your blood
It's a salt-water addiction that can never be cured
There are no Betty Ford Centers for die-hard surfers
This 'Life of Wave Riding' can run havoc on an ordinary life…
but who wants ordinary

+++

Endless layers of jungle jade run amuck
The wave I'm searching, is just down this sandy trail
I trek on

+++

There it is!
A change in the air, the scent, the sound
I can feel it, I'm close!

And, from the flora, and onto the shore of the ocean

Bleach white is the sand, sapphire blue is the sea

The salt-water blessing, and an easy-going me!

THE FATHERLAND

"Dad…Dad"
   from the opposite shore of the lake

"Dad!"

A young boy calling to his father
   not a shout of desperation,
   just trying to catch his dad's attention

"Dad!"

It rang true with me
   A sensitive skip of my heartbeat
   An overwhelming rush of emotions

From inward,
   visions of my son calling for me
   my daughter needing my being attentive
Flooding thoughts of their childhood fill me
I almost tear up
I do tear up

"Dad!"

And then, there I am, calling-out, to my own father
   an altered sentiment
   a different echo
   the tone, modified
Different from the way my children would express my presence
A parent hears that sound in another place
   an altered perspective
   an exuberant life memory

"Dad!"

Visions and memories of two souls surrounding my heart, my spirit

There she is
  kitten in her arms
  posing and smiling
  letting me know,
    Dad, this is all part of your world

And the beach walk
  a surf check
  his arm rests on my shoulder.

"Dad!"

THE FIRST MUSIC

I wonder, as you may
When did the first sound of music fill the air?
When did our Universe incorporate music and musicians?

Of course, nature's symphony forever applauded the world
The birds sang, creeks flowed, thunder roared
But music itself, from a hum, or whistle, or voice, or a drum tap
When did mankind first want to imitate, or join in harmony, or enhance
nature?
Or expand one's soul, mind, and world by creating music?

Perhaps, one tapped a wooden stick to the ground a few times and a beat
began Unconsciously, but it began
The sound was repeated: tapping, beating…drumming
Soon, another from the tribe echoed the beat?
Man marveled at the sound

Perhaps a woman loved the distant call of a bird,
and she vocalized to copy that resonance
She realized that she loved the sound that came forth from her own throat
Soon, she sang every chance she could
She would never stop singing

And, when was the first musical instrument made, and used to enhance life?
I do not know any of these answers, as you don't
But the visions are entertaining to ponder
So many possibilities

Music is forever being created, every instant
Precisely at this second!
Like grains of sand forever becoming more grains of sand
Music lives, as does those that create it.

THE FIRST DANCE

one soul
one saint
shaman
student and teacher
gathering momentum

a woman
a man
the first lean,
that first slender movement
the torso breathing the magic
the hips, and the sway, the swing
   rolling back, and forth
   and again, once more

the motion feels true
   the movement, so natural
so together, within the music

It was then, the Universe unfolded...
   to include, The First Dance

THE LAKE AT SUNSET

There, on the surface of the lake,
where the trees touch the water's edge,
   a steady breeze dances across the surface

Behind the shadowy wetness,
   the wind touches, and tickles the leaves of each tree
How many shades of green can one visualize?

The quaking of Aspens
   each leaf, *chimes…Zen Bells*
Behind this, a sacred silence,
   and with no effort, I easily launch the mind, and the soul

Oh, to feel such presence in this Divine Temple!
It's all here, visible to me, within me
   among the sounds and scents
   moving within the realm of all color
I am free…

+++

The sun's last fading presence passes behind the hill
Above this rich expanse of water, the dazzling planet of gold struggles to say
goodbye

Just a little longer, it whispers…

There it is…still awake…between the hill top trees
Then lowering its peaking orb,
   making a playground of sky so brilliant,
   so intense,
   I can't look straight toward it

I scan the multiple shores
The drowsy bays, and sandy beaches
   all resting from the day's warmth
   all, to sleep with the sun's setting salute

+++

Now, ever so slight, the cool of night, like an ebb tide, touches the eternal
circle

Quieter now

Can that be, more stillness
Yes, only to whisper in silence, it is so

THE LAKE WITH FULL MOON

Moonlit, in softness, and in shadows

  the night sky smiles down on me with pages of stars

    all gathered together to celebrate a never-ending circle

Here, I rest, gathering in the depth of the brilliance

  cozy in the bosom of the night

    free with life, and visions

Traveling on a heavenly bridge of light, the unleashed kiss of nature

  so profound and limitless,

    flaunts no farewells, no distant memories

Here, in this existing light of a full moon, I am flush with wonder!

VALLEY OF THE MOON

Running Wolf searched the summer sky for moon fire

Whispered words gave guidance and clarity

And through the mist, looking toward heaven, echoes offered credence

+

Beyond any embrace, beyond everlasting, the tribe healed itself

Souls walked the summer rains, and the sigh of the moon granted faith

+

Midnight was the sweetest for reflection

And, with their arms open wide, the tribe gathered

New souls were seized with a conquering handshake

WHATEVER GETS YOU THROUGH THE NIGHT!

Meditation
  medication
   masturbation
whatever helps you get through the night
I can see nothing wrong with it

Get naked
  get naughty
   get noisy
Relish in it, and ease through those dark hours

A good book
  deep breathing
   or burning one
I say, indulge

The tossing and turning, it's not worth the time
Just don't worry about it, relax through it all
Time to take care of, Numero Uno!

My choice, well…
Intimacy with a stunning woman
Totally wild and uninhibited lovemaking
Then, to snuggle up with this cherished femme,
   and to spoon together in the comfort that only lovers appreciate

Oh, how sensual saturation is hard to surpass!
The femme spirit, is so stirring!

Though, this evening, after all is said and done
At this nocturnal hour,
      here I am, all alone
Just here, by my lonesome, and I can't sleep

I guess it'll be a hot bath
I'll then, scribble down a few stanzas about getting through the night

SLEEP, AND SOMETIMES SNOORING

Sometimes,
    I am quiet
        like a *Heron*, the sea bird
            standing still, by the water's edge
                in the cool of the night
                    patiently waiting for a fish

Sometimes,
    I am noisy
        like the crash
            of the thunder gods
                in the dark of midnight
                    a captured jaguar

Sometimes,
    when my snoring upsets you
        please, don't startle me with an alarming shake,
            wake me with a velvety kiss

WRITTEN

passages of poetry
   read
      recited
         treasured
and, forgotten, only to become history

years pass, and the gift of a book
a present from that inner circle of dear friends
time to share what they held prized for so long a time

a book that is filled with poetry
poems that open the heart, and with a sensitive stirring, open more hearts

reflections of an author
stanzas that make the soul awaken
and there, in that moment, they are revealed
like a stream, you bathe in, and satiated, you absorb the essence
like art, we rally in it

to recite a poem
to read passages of colored verses
   and words emerge,
   elegantly,
   full with depth and truth

the book, the connection

THE MUSE

BELLA

Bella, speak to me in the language of love

Let us drift into this mystic dream,
and surround our dance with enchantment

Let's awake in the place of all shining magic
There, we will race free across the river stones

We shall soar within our sanctuary of tenderness,
the way all colors collide

You and I will kiss the song of all searching hearts
We will inherit the heavens, embrace paradise together
Forever and beyond this everlasting mystery

This truth has no option but to break loose,
and skyward, together, we shall fly!

ASIA

A delicate silk sarong
   falls with envy over your jeweled hips
Movement enhances the pleasure of seeing you glide toward me
Graceful
   like the jade of your reclusive necklace
just so, hidden from its radiance
   to blossom and rage like the exotic flower that you are

Mystic Princess,
Escape with me
We will journey to the far horizon
   for this parade of night
   for this longing, and the fire

Distant mountains only dream of your shadow
Your handprint has pierced my heart
   heart of hearts

Kiss me,
let your lips brush the substance of my enchantment
Unearth the mosaic of my abduction

Like naked poetry
   dancing
I abandon all for this embrace
Always Asia

ADRIFT

My love, lie still within my arms
Let our lips touch, and pass across time

We will walk on air
homesick no more
   among mysteries, and within heaven

Departed from the search,
   the lost sand dune of wishes will disperse
   rescued of candlelight, and secrets

Our tender embrace declares that you are now safe in my arms
No one loves you as I

Here, there are no messages to unravel
   no scattered storms of silence
   no scented distant memories
     only bays of passion, and shores of oblivion

My love, lie still within my arms
Let our lips touch, and pass across time

AUTUMN

Your autumn legs surround me
Oh, the sweetness of this encompassing embrace

My treasure,
now is our season of trance
A festival of two hearts
    held tight
    sharing the world, wherever our world

Your skilled autumn legs of love
    Calming my ache for a mirror image
    awakening the lingering sunrise of my longing
    and after, to escort an inspired heartbeat

Abanquet of morning secrets a bound by autumn legs
They launch a delicate yearning
    only to slowly cascade down upon the shore of your mystic horizon

Autumn elegance,
bend your life over my chest
sing the diamonds clear
Fortunes gather like emeralds across your skin
    browned by radiance
    sun swept pollen

Graceful, ripened legs of autumn

Indian summer of autumn!

ENCHANTRESS

Angel Midnight
   embracing my barren soul
      coloring my voyage through a veil of neon lights

Such dreams of eternal magic
   magnificent seductive dreams

From the depth of time,
   from some lonely space of disappearance,
   I emerged scarred and wounded

Only to awake, and to dream no more

Oh, how I have hungered!

CAPTURED

As the fever of your essence rages on,
my existence is seized in the pleasure of your fire

Like the fury of an ocean wave rushing and rising upon my life,
I tumble out of control from the surge
Diving headfirst into this carousel of sweet candy!

Captured within this nocturnal paradise, lust flourishes eternal

DANCING DARK MIDNIGHT

Summer

One summer night
   rising from our bed
we walked, hand in hand
   onto the thick grass
a warm lazy midnight met us there
even then, the day's heat gently lingered
we were drunk from making love

We floated together in ecstasy
  swaying
  naked
  always naked
scented honey clinging to our skin
moving with night

Our dance floor
  the August lawn

The night dancing became a ritual
our gathering
our evening engagements
no one else ever knew
we kept it a secret, always
  why share this with others

We danced through a youthful moon
  waxing
    full
      and waning moons
all summer
we were originals

Autumn

You are asleep in my arms, this November of any year
late afternoon, and an Autumn evening is already settling in upon us
this time
   wrapped as one, feels so truthful
   such a comfortable moment being with you
we are happy
   our seasons are one connected poem

ever so often
   I daydream about the heat of those summer nights
   I do miss our secret dance floor romance

If you awaken toward midnight
wake me with kiss
let's dance again

Winter

The air, so cold, stings our cheeks as we walk through another February
your coat has you covered from head to boot
I can hardly feel your body amid so many layers of cotton and fleece
Somewhere, in between a hurried walk to get out of the cool biting wind,
    you whisper how you long for summertime
for a brief second,
   we both escape to a dark lawn covered in moonlight
   covered in scented smiles
we assure each other that we will again celebrate our summer dance

Let's get home,
   turn on the heater, make it toasty
     and undress each other

Spring

We've made reservation to rent our summer cottage
  it's a distance from here
  only we know the way to get to there
  only we understand the dance we share

Our summer nights
  And Dancing Dark Midnight!

DECORATED

I admire that tattoo
   covering the sweet innocence of your castle

intriguing
I would like to see where it starts,
        and where it ends
  where it buds,
    blooms
       and
    where it begs

its origin
    at your delicate wrist
if so, does it finish on your dreamy thigh

perhaps it begins
     slowly
  sweeping
     from that small tummy
  golden and glorious
     around
to accommodating hips
  across
to the valley of your alluring sunrise

or its creation
  at the silky base of the serpent's spine
brushed and bending
skyward
slowly
  resting its hands gently
    along the side of your sleek silhouette

breathe
    gentle pastel
that shaded skin
colored in whispers of sin and spice
echoes a convincing sigh
bestowing hues of wisdom

I long to slide my lips over your dragon fire,
    and taste the magic of your colors

EARTH FLOWER

At the dawning, the crescent moon began to slowly fade
    giving way to the birth of day
The morning's glow, ever so faint,
    gently teased,
      the darkness had no choice but to surrender its grasp
My true direction appeared in these early hours

I navigated a lonely prairie that soon gave way to a pathway
    hidden from most,
      those who would not be searching
A clearing emerged,
    and there, a shining of pearls and jade arose

I ensued deeper, and about me, a mysterious garden appeared
I did not recognize this kingdom
My footsteps led me upon an intriguing flower
A Wild Rose was its companion, as was an Orchid

This blossom was so unique,
    its rapture, pristine in nature,
      appearing to be cultivated by some divine essence

I knelt, inspecting the delicate bud
Its lips, plump and blooming, flaunted fantasy
I discovered its mystic petals, violet and pink, were flush with fragrance
Exotic whites fluttered in harmony at its center
Here, each subtle hue flourished in luminous clusters of invitation

Charmed and mesmerized, as if under a hypnotic spell,
   I felt as if I commenced to rise above the mundane world
   I began to ascend to a more noble persuasion,
     one of truth and sincerity

I realized, I could never abandon this flower
This gallant gift, guide and ally,
   this friend and companion,
     This Woman

Given a wiser path, one of fulfillment
My searching ceased,
    I embraced life anew!

EMPRESS WILD!

Empress,
  such a wild bounty of earth
You possess a mad appetite for loving
With that smile, and your feverish desire,
  you have hunted

My Tigress, you are circling your prey
  and now leap into my summer!
With no mercy, you lunge upon my universe!
Such, your longing for pleasure!

Sweet Venus,
I am so eager!
I long for the taste of your lips
I so ache to embrace each gem of your storm!

Oh, I am so anticipating this lustful celebration!
I am burning,
    Rock me!
        Shake me!
            Fuck me!

Captured and overwhelmed,
  I am spinning from this excess!
The blood and breath of my being is devoured
All that was tangible in my life has now been engulfed in fire!

Here and now,
  consumed and contented,
  I've become a most satisfied victim

As in a dream, I prowl within a cave of intoxication
Lost in splendor
Staggering in your bewitched kingdom!

WILD MOUNTAIN HONEY!

Like a queen bee
   you embody the essence of all women!

And from the hive of your primal gift to me…
      I lick, and I suck this creamy swollen richness!

Your satiated spark of feminine seduction,
   this enraged radiance,
      this blossom of plush elegant indulgence!

It's all so arousing!

So famished, and so eager
   I can't stop nourishing myself on your flower!

I've never tasted anything so erotic, and so satisfying!

FLAMES OF MYTHICAL MAGIC

Lover, it's so obvious
I'm only here as a diversion
Solely included to calm your appetite to be wicked
Just that, a blanket of flattery to entertain your desires
Recruited to deliver whatever is necessary to get you through the darkness
Is that it, just here to arouse you, Princess?

And I, in heated fury, eagerly volunteering to be the solution of your craving,
   attempting to calm your desperate need for affection,
   applauding your reckless appeasement to be ravaged,
   rejoicing in your remedy for loneliness,
only to recognize my own drunken desire to be saturated in love and lust!

I've become obsessed,
   no, even more,
      shackled, and crazed within these sweet flames of healing!
Wild inside this sphere of fiery magic!

     Bound in Enraged Flames of Mythical Magic!

HAUNTED MIDNIGHT

Haunted Midnight, your voice beckoned through the warm wind
And with your arms open wide, you revealed perfect truth
I crave this memory, being anywhere near you

Oh, how I hunger for your kiss!

Like Marco Polo, my destiny is to have traveled so far a distance
To have been so close
To discover your circle of strength, and to be included your magic

Regardless of how the river runs, I won't forget my voyage to your soul
Oh, to bathe in the siren's enchanted water!

My angel, sing a lullaby, one with a happy ending
Let your song ring with promise

Heart of hearts, press your lips to mine
Kiss me… and with your kiss, whisper words of forever love

My midnight dream, never let go of my heart!

Oh, how I hunger for your kiss!

LOVE SONG

Sweetened by sea and salt
   woven in sand and thunder
     lingering for years of nights
The sharpened blue edge of glass is persuaded,
 and softens to a tender touch
     tossed smooth and legendary
       becoming the birth of a calming stone
         polished, and absorbed

This night mist of emotions that our breath shares
Adrift, floating out to sea
   bound by a caressing brush
    flush with a harvest of mystery

Only together among rivers and skies
Colored with your scarlet blood kisses
   we will fly
   soaring with grace through shadows
    through light
Scattering the night with a rosebush of whispers
       truths and twilight promises

An April spring gathers at your mouth
There, I am caressed
   inflaming a sweetened life

Oh, My Salted Mermaid
  My Infinite
  This exploration has now brought me to the tender truth

Passion's warm waves roll over my senses
Moist with the abyss of love's morning
    as the pagan dew envelops the expanse of your skin and scent
      fragrant with dusk and dawn

As the rose becomes the love song for our season

MO

I love when you shout for more

 yes, I begin to soar

and if that's not enough

 you are most beautiful in the buff

SYRENS

They are everywhere,

   clustered among waves and shores, ponds and gardens

Graciously strolling through meadows, and our minds

Cleverly handing out a shimmering of hope and happiness

They call with seductive whispers

   daring us to join their dance

We echo our response,

   and swim out to sea whatever the danger,

   how ever sharp the dagger

Embracing what we most desire

   The magic!

SUN AND SEA ROMANCE

our hypnosis bathed in sea salt
  we've become unwrapped
  bound in a soul quest
this is our sacred testament to what a love, bathed in rouge, proposes

here again, I am at the beginning
this destined grasp of love
like the brightest of suns squeezing out beyond a dark shadowy cloud
the gallant and the warmth of craving starting to encircle my heart

there is a tempest in the temple
  a bee lost in the nectar
  and with that, a new frontier to explore

sweetheart,
let's embellish the sensation
Let's turn up the volume
what do we have to lose, a good night's sleep?
we can sleep tomorrow!

I believe we should garnish the air with impending delight
let's divulge all our hidden desires
indulge in some uninhibited cavorting!
trample all our senses with primeval feasting!

we will be pilgrims of longing, setting our shimmering footprints on new soil
and finally, with clenched fists, we will scream at the gods!
we shall savor this sweet liberation
we will sanctify all with the strength of love's euphoria

THE DANCE

Dear lady
you flirt with me
I am attracted,
  mesmerized,
    and so ready for all abandonment of logic
I surrender

Please, my sugary treat
  tell me,
I need to know, is this a game?
Does this mean anything to you?

Let's make it easy
If this is the latter,
I give up
I just won't go there
  such a waste of time
  such an invasion of my life joy

If this is seduction,
  let us move on to the next step
  let me kiss your neck
  explore the temptation of soft skin
    and even further,
      for more of your magic

And you,
  don't stop what you do so well
  go ahead
  amaze me

Let us become wild
  like animals,
  those that shriek and howl
    nudging
    biting and clawing
It's all part of this the wild game
    this encompassing aphrodisiac,
    nature's dance

Well dear
Shall we hold on to one another?
  kiss with satisfying hunger
if not,
wave good bye
I'm dancing out of here

THE DAWN OF VENUS

Here, in the air of thunder,
    we unlock a sunrise of temptation
In this theater of passion,
    your Savanna lipstick serenades my life
And from behind a gentle veil, your Venus aura arises

Oh My Tigress, I love our lustful ballet
Our surrender to the sweet urgency of want
Our rendezvous of silk and senses!

The heights we aspire too!
Our plunge into the bonfire of flesh thievery!
There will be no end to this pageant of love!

An infinite sky will open
    Heaven will shake
        Our palace will be inflamed!

This will be the ledge we are meant to fall from
And we shall fall into contented soothing oblivion
This is where we replenish the heartbeat of life!

Standing mythically proud, like Mars,
    I will be the fire rhapsody that unlocks the origin of Venus

THE GET AWAY

This desolate land of sand and rocks
such a fence line of insignificance
This mandolin of time just plays on, and on

I have an idea, let's turn some heads
We need to start dancing when no one else is dancing
Let's increase the volume, the emotions, and the sensations

We've been working so hard, and too long
So many clouds across the sky
contours and contours of clouds, shading the silhouette of our affection

We need a get away!
Not our local restaurant, a movie, be back home and packed in for the night!

Come on, let's freak-out a little!
An adventure, and one that's far away from our daily grind!

Yes, a holiday away from everything and everybody
Let's go someplace we're not familiar…
Bora Bora sure echoes, "Fantastically, far away!"

With straw hats, and just about naked, we'll stretch out in the sun
We will be lazy, and love it!

No phones, no mail, no bills
No tiresome commute to work

Every few hours we'll wander to our tropical fare to get out of the heat
We'll end up twirling our swimsuits over the end of the bed post,
and, we'll explore the intimate touch again

Sweetheart, we need to get foolishly wild!
One night, let's drink too much tequila, and get crazy!

Oh, my dear one, we need to rediscover each other
We need to rekindle our friendship, our priorities, our love affair

I fear that if we don't recharge our bond, our next vacation will be solo
laying in the sun, all by ourselves

I don't want that
I want us

Yes, my love, tropical Bora Bora
let's do this, and now!

THE VOICE OF VALENTINA

This afternoon hike unearths a blue sky of promise
Pines of shining silver are decorated in pastels
Brushed with beauty, your canvas is a collage of silk and emotions

Dream sky, from here, I get a good view of the canyon
I gaze at your brilliance as it touches the water's edge
The sun's reflection sets a glow upon the creek in which you play

This burning vision is illuminated in gold
Adorned flush, with swirling circles of astral light…this electric liquid is
lavish

Oh, it's the saintly height of your splendor of why I love you so
Such finesse as your unveiling becomes an inflamed dance of spring

The passion of the season, revealed so clearly

THE WILD SIDE!

My sweet love, you are a star within an impassioned sky

Like an emerald exalted in paradise, you're my comet of fire
Like a sunbeam of promise, you're my bridge to the wild side of heaven

The flesh and spirit of your essence is scented in a gem of magnetism
This gift you share, is flattered sweet in milk and honey

My Muse
Here and now, I allow my soul to melt with yours
I surrender, and relinquish my heart to you, and to this wild side heaven!

Forever, this wild side of heaven!

TO SING

It's fine if you believe in reincarnation,

    I respect your space

I don't believe in reincarnation,

    but just in case,

    and I am reborn again,

    and as a man,

I desire to come back with an impressive voice

    one with tone and resonance,

    one with machismo!

I want to sing love songs to women

TREASURE

My Sweet
We will press our bodies together
   and in elation,
we will burn in the fury, and the glory of love

Only together, within the day's expanse
   of midnights, untamed and true
In the deserted hours of morning,
   we will uncover the path to the treasure

TURQUOISE KISS

Turquoise
Blue stone of ancient fables
how it hangs from your body
It glorifies you

The embrace
The one that took me by surprise
hypnotic as the eternal sky
Turquoise evermore

Kiss me once
   and again, once more
Drench me in a shower of wonders
My passage, filled with rushing rivers of passion
   carry me, and plunge my emotions from shore to shore
   to the shore of the infinite

River boulders of self
   lodged for decades
   hidden from expressing the longing
flattered and released
liberated
boundless
      limitless

My Jewel,
So vivid, so revealing
I rest on the warm side of your shadow
I worship in the light of your smile

Exhausted,
   exposed and exalted
I awake within this turquoise indulgence

Turquoise Evermore

YOU SEE ME LIKE NO OTHER

Your eyes are my gift, forever and beyond
Deep gems, that glow in endless beauty
Rooted, and entranced in gravity, giving birth to magic

Your eyes, hypnotize like a silken heaven
Lavish and warm, is the passion of your embrace

Goddess, you are my distant star
Snow-white, in gown of beauty

You touch my beating heart

You see me like no other

UNDAUNTED

From the fire of you stirring rose,
    I am compelled to return,
    and to return again
    even, after the great storm of emotions
    and the barren desert of separation
I return

You are the river of my life,
    the stars of my sky, my air to breathe
My magnet of longing, and ache,
    my contentment

You carry the laughter, and the tears
Oh, how we laughed and cried,
    bursting in spewing truth
You're the one who accepted me as I am, when others would not
Always my friend to counsel and encourage
You are the attentive step when I am hesitant
    the forest of my serenity, the taste of temptation

I can't conceal my thirst to be swept up in your tenderness,
    so rich in feminine charm
For the blend of your scents and secrets
For the colorful expanse of your presence
    true in scarlet and in grey

I am never without you
    in mist, or sunlight,
    in reflection, or in whispers of moonlight
You are the midnight of caresses
    the song of my heart
My tempest, the siren of poetry
    the echo in my mirror

Like the Black Forest Calla, creamy in burgundy blooms,
  your ocean is deep with miracles to behold

It's the escape to your arms that initiates my arrival at the doorstep

To be at your mouth, and at your heartbeat
  resting safe from the haunts of all hearts
Creating more warmth then a thousand tropic nights
  long in feasting
And so penetrating is your persuasion,
that my thread of passage is easily laced with sin and smiles

Lover, I never know what to expect from your hungering
I love your surprise, your savage honey
We share a fertile spice that others only dream

Oh, how I hunger to confide in the heat of our melting bodies,
  and then, to rest in the calm of distant planets,
  or the raindrops of clenched fists
Only to disappear in the soft harmony of affection
  secure in the fondness of our friendship

Undaunted, you are my impulsive star soaring through my night

Yours, is the rousing soul that is the rhythm of my life

THE SPOKEN WORD

This last spring, I had the valuable experience to share some of my poetry at a local wine bar. The opportunity to gather with like-minded folks (the tribe), and stand together sharing in stories and prose had been entertaining and enlightening. So heading to the mountains for the summer, I was determined to find more venues for mixing it up with other writers.

After settling in to my Sierra retreat, such a setting presented itself. I discovered that it was open mic night for poets and musicians at a fairly hip restaurant, so I sign up to recite.

This evening, a crowd of about twenty applauded everyone that preceded me. Truthfully, I wasn't all that impressed with one fellow that struggled to sing a couple of his original songs. And two of the 'first time authors' shyly reading their poetry, didn't having me swooning. But I was happy for all that presented their work, and honored with the fact that they were brave enough to recite their pieces and sing their songs. Bravo! I'm sure their next time to share their creativity the value will rise dynamically.

The evening carries on, and I feel my entrance to recite is approaching. Well, I'm wrong, as two more musicians are invited to the stage to share their music. After those two entertain the crowd, I think, "I must be next"? But I am delayed once again as another woman is called upon to begin her set of music. And what a set of music! She starts her performance with some explosive rock and roll, really down and dirty, kick-ass rock! I mean, she's hitting it, and the place is jumping! She's good, and her stage presence is very professional.

I should also point out that she had been accompanied to the gig with an entourage, and her friends are exceptionally encouraging! They are ecstatically dancing around the restaurant's stage to each song she's performing! As this musician finishes one of her numbers, she jumps right into another! And each song is getting louder and more up-tempo. The place is cooking!

To add to the situation, instead of a short, two-song set, this woman is into her sixth song when she finally gets the hint from the announcer that she's Bogarting the stage. She finishes her last number to a loud round of applause and yells for more! "Encore" they are shouting! She strolls back to her girlfriends completely pleased with her fiery set of music. Back at her table, her friends are in an emotional frenzy about her stage time.

The MC gets to the microphone and hoots about her performance! He then quietly whispers, "And now, here's Lorenzo Lago". Actually, you really can't hear my name being announced clearly because the last performer's group is in full party mode.

I walk up to the microphone and introduce myself. The crowd now does their best to be respectful, quiets down, and gives me their attention. I begin, and recite a short poem…and the audience doesn't respond. They don't get it!

The patrons are attentive, but no real recognition of what I'm trying to convey to them. I know this isn't working, and sense that this is a terrible time to share my words.

Just as I start another poem, and from somewhere deep inside the bowels of the kitchen, an annoying sound of a dishwashing machine begins to resonate throughout the restaurant.

I have to begin again, and I speak louder! It now seems like the dishwashing machine and I are competing for the audience's attention…and I'm losing! After reciting one line of poetry, I stop, grin and laugh. I then step away from the microphone, and leave the stage. I walk to the table I had been sitting, pick up my beer, and take a strong swig. Another musician has now taken the stage, and begins to belt out a Credence Clearwater Revival song.

The venue's MC walks over to me and asks why I spent such a short amount of time on stage. I quietly tell him he should have had me on before the 'rock and roller'. He seems to understand, but we both know that there's not much we can do about that now. I drain my beer, and walk out of the place.

As I climb into my car, I think how happy I am that won't ever be on that stage again! I mean, I am so pleased that the whole exasperating fiasco is over! I also realize that this evening's experience has been perfect for my ego. Geez, another good lesson in life! One may anticipate that an audience will hang on every syllable I utter, but not so. What stirs my soul may, may not have any prevalence with others. Who knows, maybe it's all about timing. Or, venue's atmosphere. Or, how the planets are aligned? Chuckling, I whisper, "The world loves to throw us a curve!"

As I drive back home, I decide to swing by the lake for a look. The sun just set, and there's still the colorful 'evening light' in this June sky.

I pull my vehicle into an empty parking lot, turn off the engine, and step out of the car into the evening tranquility. I then walk to the edge of the lake, and become part of the stillness that is now surrounding me.

No sounds fill this space, no people talking, and no barking dogs to disrupt this serenity. All I hear and perceive is the constant, soothing sound of the Universe unfolding in front of me, and in all its dignified glory!

An afterglow of radiant cobalt blue fills the sky at the far side of the lake. A warm darkness spreads out from there into the distance. I pull off what clothes I am wearing, and step into the lake's warm water. I roll over on my back, and I float free of any microphones and audiences. I drift, gliding upon the lake's surface, released of any personal issues about sharing my poetry. In this setting, and at this moment in time, I'm in total peace with what stirs my heart, and my soul.

I just float, naked, eyes open wide, staring up, and toward a vast parade of infinite abundance.

www.ingramcontent.com/pod-product-compliance
Lightning Source LLC
Chambersburg PA
CBHW081333090426
42737CB00017B/3116